The Little Book of Leadership Wisdom

By

CHARLES D. HARPOOL

The Little Book of Leadership Wisdom
Copyright © 2014 Charles D. Harpool
All Rights Reserved
Printed in the United States of America
ISBN 10: 149228937X
ISBN 13: 9781492289371
Library of Congress Control Number: 2013916029
CreateSpace Independent Publishing Platform
North Charleston, South Carolina

No part of *The Little Book of Leadership Wisdom* may be reproduced, stored in a retrieval system, or transmitted, in any form or by any means, without prior permission in writing from the author, or as expressly permitted by law, or under terms agreed with the appropriate reprographics rights organization. Enquiries concerning reproduction outside of the scope above should be e-mailed to cdharpool@gmail.com.

All scripture quotations are taken from the THE HOLY BIBLE, NEW INTERNATIONAL VERSION®, NIV® Copyright © 1973, 1978, 1984, 2011 by Biblica, Inc.™ Used by permission. All rights reserved worldwide.

Dedication

To my Lord and savior, Jesus Christ.

To my wife Barbara, and our daughter, Christine, who enrich and bless my life in countless ways every day

To my parents, Charles and Virginia Harpool, who were the best parents in the world.

To my in-laws, Larry and June Buffington, who were the best in-laws in the world.

To my twin brother, Dennis Harpool, who was brilliant and left us far too soon.

To my younger brother Doug Harpool.

To my younger twin brothers, David and Darryl Harpool.

To my lifelong best friend, Don Evans.

Contents

	Introduction	vii
	Acknowledgments	ix
1	Leadership Wisdom from the Bible	1
2	Leadership Wisdom from Philosophers	9
3	Leadership Wisdom from Presidents and World Leaders	19
4	Leadership Wisdom from Military Leaders	33
5	Leadership Wisdom from Business Leaders	43
6	Leadership Wisdom from Sports Figures	75
7	Leadership Wisdom from Literature and the Arts	83
8	Leadership Wisdom from Scientists and Inventors	99
9	Leadership Wisdom from Proverbs	109
10	Other Leadership Wisdom	115
	Index	125
	About the Author	133

Introduction

Are leaders born or made? What are the common personality traits and characteristics of great leaders? What is the best definition of leadership? These are important leadership questions that have been studied and debated for centuries. *The Little Book of Leadership Wisdom* does not end the debate on these key leadership questions, but it will help you become a better leader.

All leaders know that leadership is rewarding, but leadership can also be challenging. My mission for *The Little Book of Leadership Wisdom* is to help both new, and experienced leaders, be more effective. *The Little Book of Leadership Wisdom* contains leadership wisdom and motivation from over 185 diverse sources. These gems of leadership wisdom are selected from the Bible, philosophers, presidents, business, sports figures, scientists, literature, arts, proverbs, world and military leaders.

The Little Book of Leadership Wisdom will inform, entertain, challenge and motivate you to become a better leader. It is a valuable resource that will provide a great return on investment for the time you spend reading and contemplating these gems of leadership wisdom.

"I quote others only in order the better to express myself."

— Michel de Montaigne

Acknowledgments

I want to acknowledge my wife for her support and encouragement for this project and my daughter for her editing assistance and contributions to the book. Thank you to all the organizations who have allowed me to be a part of their leadership teams throughout my business career. A special thank you to all the people I have had the privilege of leading.

I want to acknowledge Dick Kampa, Gene Fortson, and the late Dr. Joe B. Hatcher, who have been great mentors to me. They are great examples of leadership and leading by example. They have generously shared their leadership wisdom and helped me become a better leader.

The quotations included in *The Little Book of Leadership Wisdom* represent the author's choices and his desire to share a variety of perspectives. Every attempt was made to credit the original authors of the quotations and to quote them accurately.

"The wisdom of the wise and the experience of the ages are perpetuated by quotations."
—Benjamin Disraeli

Chapter 1

Leadership Wisdom from the Bible

The Little Book of Leadership Wisdom

Not looking to your own interests, but each of you to the interests of the others.

NIV, Philippians 2:4

Cast all your anxiety on him because he cares for you.

NIV, 1 Peter 5:7

He must become greater; I must become less.

NIV, John 3:30

Let us not become weary in doing good, for at the proper time we will reap a harvest if we do not give up.

NIV, Galatians 6:9

Leadership Wisdom from the Bible

I can do all this through him who gives me strength.
>NIV, Philippians 4:13

Do to others as you would like them to do to you.
>NIV, Luke 6:31

Do nothing out of selfish ambition or vain conceit. Rather, in humility value others above yourselves.
>NIV, Philippians 2:3

Above all else, guard your heart, for everything you do flows from it.
>NIV, Proverbs 4:23

The Little Book of Leadership Wisdom

But select capable men from all the people—men who fear God, trustworthy men who hate dishonest gain—and appoint them as officials over thousands, hundreds, fifties, and tens.

NIV, Exodus 18:21

And David shepherded them with integrity of heart; with skillful hands he led them.

NIV, Psalms 78:72

Be shepherds of God's flock that is under your care, watching over them—not because you must, but because you are willing, as God wants you to be; not pursuing dishonest gain, but eager to serve; not lording it over those entrusted to you, but being examples to the flock.

NIV, 1 Peter 5:2-3

Before a downfall the heart is haughty, but humility comes before honor.

NIV, Proverbs 18:12

Leadership Wisdom from the Bible

…All of you, clothe yourselves with humility toward one another, because, "God opposes the proud but gives grace to the humble."

NIV, 1 Peter 5:5

Speak up for those who cannot speak for themselves, for the rights of all who are destitute. Speak up and judge fairly; defend the rights of the poor and needy.

NIV, Proverbs 31:8-9

Remember your leaders, who spoke the word of God to you. Consider the outcome of their way of life and imitate their faith.

NIV, Hebrews 13:7

Teach me to do your will, for you are my God; may your good Spirit lead me on level ground.

NIV, Psalms 143:10

The Little Book of Leadership Wisdom

Call to me and I will answer you and tell you great and unsearchable things, which you do not know.
>NIV, Jeremiah 33:3

Each of you should use whatever gift you have received to serve others, as faithful stewards of God's grace in its various forms.
>NIV, 1 Peter 4:10

Get wisdom, get understanding; do not forget my words or turn away from them.
>NIV, Proverbs 4:5

And we know that in all things God works for the good of those who love him, who have been called according to his purpose.
>NIV, Romans 8:28

Leadership Wisdom from the Bible

The beginning of wisdom is this: Get wisdom...
>NIV, Proverbs 4:7

Where there is no revelation, people cast off restraint; but blessed is the one who heeds wisdom's instruction.
>NIV, Proverbs 29:18

Pray that the LORD your God will tell us where we should go and what we should do.
>NIV, Jeremiah 42:3

...whoever wants to be great among you must be your servant.
>NIV, Matthew 20:16

Chapter 2

Leadership Wisdom from Philosophers

The Little Book of Leadership Wisdom

The best is he who calls men to the best. And those who heed the call are also blessed. But worthless who call not, heed not, but rest.

> Hesiod

Leadership does not depend upon being right.

> Ivan Illich

The crowd gives the leader new strength.

> Evenius

He who has never learned to obey cannot be a good commander.

> Aristotle

Leadership Wisdom from Philosophers

He who has great power should use it lightly.
> Lucius Annaeus Seneca

To know what people really think, pay regard to what they do, rather than what they say.
> George Santayana

The will to win, the desire to succeed, the urge to reach your full potential…these are the keys that will unlock the door to personal excellence.
> Confucius

To convert somebody go and take them by the hand and guide them.
> Thomas Aquinas

Knowledge is power.

> Sir Francis Bacon

All speech is vain and empty unless it be accompanied by action.

> Demosthenes

Good people do not need laws to tell them to act responsibly, while bad people will find a way around the laws.

> Plato

Let him that would move the world, first move himself.

> Socrates

Leadership Wisdom from Philosophers

Choose a job you love, and you will never have to work a day in your life.

> Confucius

Who questions much, shall learn much, and retain much.

> Sir Francis Bacon

We are what we repeatedly do. Excellence, then, is not an act, but a habit.

> Aristotle

The higher we are placed, the more humbly we should walk.

> Marcus Tullius Cicero

The Little Book of Leadership Wisdom

No one was ever great without some portion of divine inspiration.
>Marius Tullius Cicero

When it is obvious that the goals cannot be reached, don't adjust the goals; adjust the action steps.
>Confucius

The wisest mind has something to learn.
>George Santayana

Common sense is not so common.
>Voltaire

Leadership Wisdom from Philosophers

You will never do anything in this world without courage. It is the greatest quality of the mind next to honor.

Aristotle

He only employs his passion can make no use of his reason.

Marcus Tullius Cicero

When anger rises think about the consequences.

Confucius

A leader is best when people barely know he exists, when his work is done, his aim fulfilled, they will say: we did it ourselves.

Lao Tzu

The Little Book of Leadership Wisdom

The best and safest thing is to keep a balance in your life, acknowledging the great powers around us. If you can do that and live that way you are really a wise man.

Euripides

Waste of time is the most extravagant and costly of all expenses.

Theophrastus

Difficulties strengthen the mind, as labor does the body.

Lucius Annaeus Seneca

Our greatest glory is not in never falling, but in rising every time we fall.

Confucius

Leadership Wisdom from Philosophers

No man was ever made wise by chance.
                    Lucius Annaeus Seneca

The eyes are more exact witnesses than the ears.
                    Heraclitus

Good actions give strength to ourselves and inspire good actions in others.

                    Plato

Every player must accept the cards life deals him or her: but once they are in hand, he or she alone must decide how to play the cards in order to win the game.
                    Voltaire

The Little Book of Leadership Wisdom

All human actions have one or more of these seven causes: chance, nature, compulsion, habit, reason, passion, and desire.

Aristotle

Write down the thoughts of the moment. Those that come unsought for are commonly the most valuable.

Francis Bacon

It is a rough road that leads to the heights of greatness.

Lucius Annaeus Seneca

The greater the difficulty the more glory in surmounting it.

Epicurus

Chapter 3

Leadership Wisdom from Presidents and World Leaders

The Little Book of Leadership Wisdom

If your actions inspire others to dream more, learn more, do more, and become more, you are a leader.
John Quincy Adams

It is better to lead from behind and to put others in front, especially when you celebrate victory when nice things occur. You take the front line when there is danger. Then people will appreciate your leadership.
Nelson Mandela

Leadership must be established from the top down.
Sam Nunn

Don't be afraid to see what you see.
Ronald Reagan

Leadership Wisdom from Presidents and World Leaders

Leaders lead, but in the end it's the people who deliver.

Tony Blair

There is no indispensable man.

Franklin D. Roosevelt

I do the very best I know how – the very best I can; and I mean to keep on doing it until the end. Nearly all men can stand adversity, but if you want to test a man's character, give him power.

Abraham Lincoln

It is, after all, the responsibility of the expert to operate the familiar, and that of a leader to transcend it.

Henry A. Kissinger

The Little Book of Leadership Wisdom

Absolute identity with one's cause is the first and great condition of successful leadership.
> Woodrow Wilson

Always bear in mind that your own resolution to succeed is more important than any one thing.
> Abraham Lincoln

I know of no single formula for success. But over the years I have observed that some attributes of leadership are universal and are often about finding ways of encouraging people to combine their efforts, their talents, their insights, their enthusiasm and their inspiration to work together.
> Queen Elizabeth II

A leader is someone who brings people together.
> George W. Bush

Leadership Wisdom from Presidents and World Leaders

Leadership is about taking responsibility, not making excuses.

> Mitt Romney

Leadership and learning are indispensable to each other.

> John F. Kennedy

Actions speak louder than words.

> Theodore Roosevelt

Leadership to me means duty, honor, and country. It means character, and it means listening from time to time.

> George W. Bush

Faced with crisis, the man of character falls back upon himself.
>Charles de Gaulle

The best executive is the one who has sense enough to pick good people to do what he wants done, and self-restraint to keep from meddling with them while they do it.
>Theodore Roosevelt

Important principles may and must be inflexible.
>Abraham Lincoln

We live in a society obsessed with public opinion. But leadership has never been about popularity.
>Marco Rubio

Leadership Wisdom from Presidents and World Leaders

The ear of the leader must ring with the voices of the people.

> Woodrow Wilson

I must follow the people. Am I not their leader?

> Benjamin Disraeli

Within the covers of the Bible are the answers for all the problems we face.

> Ronald Reagan

The price of greatness is responsibility.

> Winston Churchill

The Little Book of Leadership Wisdom

People ask the difference between a leader and a boss. The leader leads, and the boss drives.
> Theodore Roosevelt

And so, my fellow Americans, ask not what your country can do for you, ask what you can do for your country.
> John F. Kennedy

Never take anything for granted.
> Benjamin Disraeli

The nation will find it very hard to look up to the leaders who are keeping their ears to the ground.
> Winston Churchill

Leadership Wisdom from Presidents and World Leaders

It is amazing what you can accomplish if you do not care who gets the credit.

                                        Harry S. Truman

When you can't make them see the light, make them feel the heat.

                                        Ronald Reagan

Speak softly and carry a big stick; you will go far.

                                        Theodore Roosevelt

To state the facts frankly is not to despair for the future nor indict the past.

                                        John F. Kennedy

The Little Book of Leadership Wisdom

The task of the leader is to get his people from where they are to where they have not been.

                                                  Henry A. Kissinger

---

I think leadership's always been about two main things: imagination and courage.

                                                  Paul Keating

---

Leadership does not always wear the harness of compromise.

                                                  Woodrow Wilson

---

To be able to lead others, a man must be willing to go forward alone.

                                                  Harry S. Truman

Leadership Wisdom from Presidents and World Leaders

Never…Never…Never…Never Give Up!
                                    Winston Churchill

The only limit to our realization of tomorrow will be our doubts of today.
                                    Franklin D. Roosevelt

Well done is better than well said.
                                    Benjamin Franklin

Whenever you are to do a thing, though it can never be known but to yourself, ask yourself how you would act were all the world looking at you, and act accordingly.
                                    Thomas Jefferson

The Little Book of Leadership Wisdom

The buck stops here.

> Harry Truman

It is always better to have no ideas that false ones; to believe nothing, than to believe what is wrong.

> Thomas Jefferson

We must hang together, or most assuredly, we shall hang separately.

> Benjamin Franklin

You have enemies? Good. That means you've stood up for something, sometime in your life.

> Winston Churchill

Leadership Wisdom from Presidents and World Leaders

A good leader inspires people to have confidence in the leader, a great leader inspires people to have confidence in themselves.

Eleanor Roosevelt

In matters of style, swim with the current; in matters of principle, stand like a rock.

Thomas Jefferson

Men make history and not the other way around. In periods where there is no leadership, society stands still. Progress occurs when courageous, skillful leaders seize the opportunity to change things for the better.

Harry S. Truman

Difficulties mastered are opportunities won.

Winston Churchill

Chapter 4

Leadership Wisdom from Military Leaders

The Little Book of Leadership Wisdom

Leadership is a potent combination of strategy and character. But if you must be without one, be without the strategy.

Norman Schwarzkopf

You don't lead by hitting people over the head – that's assault, not leadership.

Dwight D. Eisenhower

My own definition of leadership is this: the capacity and the will to rally men and women to a common purpose and the character which inspires confidence.

Bernard Montgomery

A competent leader can get efficient service from poor troops, while on the contrary an incapable leader can demoralize the best of troops.

John J. Pershing

Leadership Wisdom from Military Leaders

You manage things; you lead people.
>Grace Murray Hopper

Be willing to make decisions. That's the most important quality in a good leader.
>George S. Patton

The truest wisdom is a resolute determination.
>Napoleon Bonaparte

The supreme quality for leadership is unquestionably integrity. Without it, no real success is possible, no matter whether it is on a section gang, a football field, in an army, or in an office.
>Dwight D. Eisenhower

Leadership is understanding people and involving them to help you do a job. That takes all of the good characteristics, like integrity, dedication of purpose, selflessness, knowledge, skill, implacability, as well as determination not to accept failure.

> Arleigh A. Burke

Leadership consists of picking good men and helping them do their best.

> Chester W. Nimitz

Lead me, follow me, or get out of my way.

> George S. Patton

The truth of the matter is: that you always know the right thing to do. The hard part is doing it.

> Norman Schwarzkopf

Leadership Wisdom from Military Leaders

Leadership is the art of getting someone else to do something you want done because he wants to do it.

>Dwight D. Eisenhower

Few things are brought to a successful issue by impetuous desire, but most by calm and prudent thought.

>Napoleon Bonaparte

A leader is a man who can adapt principles to circumstances.

>George S. Patton

Leadership is solving problems. The day soldiers stop bringing you their problems is the day you have stopped leading them. They have either lost confidence that you can help or concluded you do not care. Either case is a failure of leadership.

>Colin Powell

The task of leadership is not to put greatness into people, but to elicit it, for the greatness is there already.

John Buchan

Leadership must be based on goodwill. Goodwill does not mean posturing and, least of all, pandering to the mob. It means obvious and wholehearted commitment to helping followers…

James B. Stockdale

A sense of humor is part of the art of leadership, of getting along with people, of getting things done.

Dwight D. Eisenhower

Never give an order that can't be obeyed.

Douglas MacArthur

Leadership Wisdom from Military Leaders

If everyone is thinking alike, then somebody isn't thinking.

George S. Patton

A true leader has the confidence to stand alone, the courage to make tough decisions, and the compassion to listen to the needs of others. He does not set out to be a leader, but becomes one by the equality of his actions and the integrity of his intent.

Douglas MacArthur

When I give a minister an order. I leave it to him to find the means to carry it out.

Napoleon Bonaparte

I will find a way, or make a way.

Hannibal Barra

The Little Book of Leadership Wisdom

Great leaders are almost always great simplifiers, who can cut through an argument, debate, and doubt to offer a solution that everybody can understand.

Colin Powell

Never tell people how to do things. Tell them what to do and they will surprise you with their ingenuity.

George S. Patton

There is nothing impossible to him who will try.

Alexander the Great

A leader is a dealer in hope.

Napoleon Bonaparte

Leadership Wisdom from Military Leaders

Always do everything you ask of those you command.
George Patton

When things go wrong in your command, start searching for the reason in increasingly larger circles around your own desk.
Bruce C. Clarke

Leadership is intangible, and therefore no weapon ever designed can replace it.
Omar N. Bradley

Every mission accomplished.
Matthew B. Ridgway

When a thing is done, it's done. Don't look back. Look forward to your next objective.
George C. Marshall

One man with courage makes a majority.
Andrew Jackson

I cannot trust a man to control others who cannot control himself.
Robert E. Lee

It is better to be alone, than to be in bad company.
George Washington

Chapter 5

Leadership Wisdom from Business Leaders

The Little Book of Leadership Wisdom

Effective leadership is not about making speeches or being liked; leadership is defined by results not attributes.

> Peter Drucker

Good leadership consists of showing average people how to do the work of superior people.

> John D. Rockefeller

A man always has two reasons for doing anything: a good reason and the real reason.

> J. P. Morgan

Innovation distinguishes between a leader and follower.

> Steve Jobs

Leadership Wisdom from Business Leaders

Management is doing things right; leadership is doing the right things.

> Peter Drucker

Leadership is simply the ability of an individual to coalesce the efforts of other individuals toward achieving common goals. It boils down to looking after your people and ensuring that, from top to bottom, everyone feels a part of the team.

> Frederick Smith

Business leaders cannot be bystanders.

> Howard Schultz

If you can provide the funding and you will get the leadership, you'll have a competitive team.

> T. Boone Pickens

The Little Book of Leadership Wisdom

My four years in the Marine Corps left me with an indelible understanding of the value of leadership skills.

Frederick Smith

And I'd say one of the great lessons I've learned over the past couple of decades, from a management perspective, is that really, when you come down to it, it really is all about people and all about leadership.

Steve Case

I think it is important for people who are given leadership roles to assume that role immediately.

Bob Iger

Honor bespeaks worth. Confidence begets trust. Service brings satisfaction. Cooperation proves the quality of leadership.

J. C. Penney

Leadership Wisdom from Business Leaders

The growth and development of people is the highest calling of leadership.
>Harvey S. Firestone

I forgot to shake hands and be friendly. It was an important lesson about leadership.
>Lee Iacocca

No institution can possibly survive if it needs geniuses or supermen to manage it. It must be organized in such a way as to be able to get along under a leadership composed of average human beings.
>Peter Drucker

Turnaround or growth, it's getting people focused on the goal that is still the job of leadership.
>Anne M. Mulcahy

The Little Book of Leadership Wisdom

What I've really learned over time is that optimism is a very, very important part of leadership.

> Bob Iger

The secret of my success is a two word answer: Know people.

> Harvey S. Firestone

You're only as good as the people you hire.

> Ray Kroc

If everyone is moving forward together, then success takes care of itself.

> Henry Ford

Leadership Wisdom from Business Leaders

Leaders grasp nettles.

> David Ogilvy

Get the best people, and train them well.

> Scott McNealy

Great companies in the way they work, start with great leaders.

> Steve Ballmer

Good enough never is.

> Debbi Fields

The Little Book of Leadership Wisdom

Making those around you feel invisible is the opposite of leadership.

Margaret Heffernan

It takes twenty years to build a reputation and five minutes to ruin it. If you think about that, you will do things differently.

Warren Buffett

The first man gets the oyster, the second man gets the shell.

Andrew Carnegie

Power should be reserved for weightlifting and boats, and leadership really involves responsibility.

Herb Kelleher

Leadership Wisdom from Business Leaders

No person will make a great business who wants to do it all himself or get all the credit.

Andrew Carnegie

Management is about arranging and telling.
Leadership is about nurturing and enhancing.

Tom Peters

When your values are clear to you, making decisions becomes easier.

Roy E. Disney

Chains of habit are too light to be felt until they are too heavy to be broken.

Warren Buffett

The Little Book of Leadership Wisdom

The quality of a leader is reflected in the standards they set for themselves.

Ray Kroc

The speed of the leader is the speed of the gang.

Mary Kay Ash

Leadership is practiced not so much in words as in attitude and in action.

Harold Geneen

You have to think anyway, so why not think big?

Donald Trump

Leadership Wisdom from Business Leaders

When the world is in the midst of change, when adversity and opportunity are almost indistinguishable, this is the time for visionary leadership and when leaders need to look beyond the survival needs of those they're serving.

Chip Conley

High expectations are the key to everything.

Sam Walton

Leadership cannot really be taught. It can only be learned.

Harold Geneen

Go as far as you can see; when you get there, you'll be able to see farther.

J. P. Morgan

Good management is the art of making problems so interesting and their solutions so constructive that everyone wants to get to work and deal with them.
                                                       Paul Hawken

---

Be a yardstick of quality. Some people aren't used to an environment where excellence is expected.
                                                       Steve Jobs

---

Face reality as it is, not as it was or as you wish it to be.
                                                       Jack Welch

---

Lead and inspire people. Don't try to manage and manipulate people. Inventories can be managed, but people must be led.
                                                       Ross Perot

Leadership Wisdom from Business Leaders

Follow effective action with quiet reflection. From the quiet reflection will come more effective action.

> Peter Drucker

Leaders don't create followers, they create more leaders.

> Tom Peters

Don't find fault, find a remedy.

> Henry Ford

The signs of outstanding leadership appear primarily among the followers. Are the followers reaching their potential? Are they learning? Serving? Do they achieve the required results? Do they change with grace? Manage conflict?

> Max De Pree

The Little Book of Leadership Wisdom

Outstanding leaders go out of their way to boost the self-esteem of their personnel. If people believe in themselves, it's amazing what they can accomplish.

Sam Walton

Good business leaders create a vision, articulate the vision, passionately own the vision, and relentlessly drive it to completion.

Jack Welch

The first responsibility of a leader is to define reality. The last is to say thank you. In between a leader is a servant.

Max De Pree

Most discussions of decision making assume that only senior executives make decisions or that only senior executives' decisions matter. This is a dangerous mistake.

Peter Drucker

Leadership Wisdom from Business Leaders

The key to successful leadership today is influence, not authority.

> Kenneth Blanchard

Leadership is much more an art, belief, a condition of the heart, than a set of things to do. The visible signs of artful leadership are expressed, ultimately, in its practice.

> Max De Pree

Its fine to celebrate success, but it's more important to heed the lessons of failure.

> Bill Gates

You can't build a reputation on what you are going to do.

> Henry Ford

The Little Book of Leadership Wisdom

Before you are a leader, success is all about growing yourself. When you become a leader, success is all about growing others.
Jack Welch

Leadership is getting people to work for you when they are not obligated.
Frederick Smith

The older I get, the less I listen to what people say, and the more I look at what they do.
Andrew Carnegie

Leadership is not magnetic personality that can just as well be a glib tongue. It is not "making friends and influencing people", that is flattery. Leadership is lifting a person's vision to higher sights, the raising of a person's performance to a higher standard, the building of a personality beyond its normal limitations.
Peter Drucker

Leadership Wisdom from Business Leaders

Management manages by making decisions and by seeing that those decisions are implemented.

Harold Geneen

The best leaders are the best note takers, best askers and best learners. They are shameless thieves.

Tom Peters

Leaders must be close enough to relate to others, but far enough ahead to motivate them.

John Maxwell

And no, we don't know where it will lead. We just know there's something much bigger than any of us here.

Steve Jobs

The Little Book of Leadership Wisdom

Don't manage: lead change before you have to.
>Jack Welch

As we look ahead into next the next century, leaders will be those who empower others.
>Bill Gates

It's really clear that the most precious resource we all have is time.
>Steve Jobs

Efficiency is doing things right; effectiveness is doing the right things.
>Peter Drucker

Leadership Wisdom from Business Leaders

Leadership is the capacity to translate vision into reality.

                                                Warren Bennis

---

Discipline is the bridge between goal and accomplishment.

                                                Jim Rohn

Most people spend more time and energy going around problems than in trying to solve them.

                                                Henry Ford

Complexity is your enemy. Any fool can make something complicated. It is hard to keep things simple.

                                                Sir Richard Branson

Time is the scarcest resource, and unless it is managed, nothing else can be managed.

> Peter Drucker

Uncertainty will always be part of the taking-charge process.

> Harold Geneen

The most dangerous leadership myth is that leaders are born—that there is a genetic factor to leadership. That's nonsense; in fact, the opposite is true. Leaders are made rather than born.

> Warren Bennis

Don't necessarily avoid sharp edges. Occasionally they are necessary to leadership.

> Donald Rumsfeld

Leadership Wisdom from Business Leaders

The chief strategist of an organization has to be the leader-the CEO.

Michael Porter

Nothing is more limiting to a group than the inability to talk about the truth.

Peter Senge

Executives owe it to the organization and to their fellow workers not to tolerate nonperforming individuals in important jobs.

Peter Drucker

Become the kind of leader that people would follow voluntarily; even if you had no title or position.

Brian Tracy

The Little Book of Leadership Wisdom

The greatest leaders mobilize others by coalescing people around a shared vision.
> Kenneth Blanchard

Leadership is action, not position.
> Donald H. McGannon

The leaders who lead most effectively, it seems to me, never say "I." And that's not because they have trained themselves not to say "I." They don't think "I." They think "we"; they think "team." They understand their job to be to make the team function. They accept responsibility and don't sidestep it, but "we" gets credit…This is what creates trust, what enables you to get the task done.
> Peter Drucker

Good leaders need a positive agenda, not just an agenda of dealing with crisis.
> Michael Porter

Leadership Wisdom from Business Leaders

A new leader has to be able to change an organization that is dreamless, soulless, and visionless…Someone's got to make the wake-up call.

Warren Bennis

Great leadership does not mean running away from reality. Sometimes the hard truths might just demoralize the company, but at other times sharing difficulties can inspire people to take action that will make the situation better.

John Kotter

Leadership is the challenge to be something more than average.

Jim Rohn

Whether you think you can or think you can't—you are right.

Henry Ford

The Little Book of Leadership Wisdom

The world has the habit of making room for the person whose words and actions show that they know where they are going.

Napoleon Hill

The challenge of leadership is to be strong, but not rude; be kind, but not weak; be bold, but not bully; be thoughtful, but not lazy; be humble, but not timid' be proud, but not arrogant; have humor, but without folly.

Jim Rohn

So much of what we call management consists of making it difficult for people to work.

Peter Drucker

In the end, you're measured not by how much you undertake, but what you finally accomplished.

Donald Trump

Leadership Wisdom from Business Leaders

Visionary leadership rather than managerial skill will be the most valued standard for tomorrow's top officer.
>Lester Korn

We have to undo a hundred year-old concept and convince our managers that their role is not to control people and stay "on top of things", but rather to guide, energize, and excite.
>Jack Welch

Nothing so conclusively proves a man's ability to lead others as what he does from day to day to lead himself.
>Thomas J. Watson

America's leaders need to put their feet in the shoes of working Americans.
>Howard Schultz

The Little Book of Leadership Wisdom

If you pick the right people and give them the opportunity to spread their wings and put compensation as a carrier behind it you almost don't have to manage them.

Jack Welch

It's not an experiment if you know it's going to work.

Jeff Bezos

The goal of an effective leader is to recondition your team to be solution focused rather than problem focused.

Jim Rohn

It's all right to be Goliath, but always act like David.

Philip Knight

Leadership Wisdom from Business Leaders

I think that my leadership style is to get people to fear staying in place, to fear not changing.
Louis Gertsner

Control is not leadership; management is not leadership; leadership is leadership. If you seek to lead, invest at least fifty percent of your time in leading yourself—your own purpose, ethics, principles, motivation and conduct.
Dee Hock

The role of leadership is to transform the complex situation into small pieces and prioritize them.
Carlos Ghosn

I think the currency of leadership is transparency. You've got to be truthful. I don't think you should be vulnerable every day, but there are moments where you've got to share your soul and conscience with people and show them who you are, and not be afraid of it.
Howard Schultz

The Little Book of Leadership Wisdom

The leadership instinct you are born with is the backbone. You develop the funny bone and the wishbone to go along with it.

Elaine Agather

Delegating work works, provided the one delegating works too.

Robert Half

If there is such a thing as good leadership, it is to give a good example. I have to do it for all the IKEA employees.

Ingvar Kamprad

Giving people self-confidence is by far the most important thing I can do because then they will act.

Jack Welch

Leadership Wisdom from Business Leaders

A business leader has to keep their organization focused on the mission. That sound easy, but it can be tremendously challenging in today's competitive and ever-changing business environment. A leader also has to motivate potential partners to join.

Meg Whitman

Leadership is hard to define and good leadership is even harder. But if you can get people to follow you to the ends of the earth, you are a great leader.

Indra Nooyi

People cannot be managed. Inventories can be managed, but people must be led.

Ross Perot

We're all working together; that's the secret.

Sam Walton

The Little Book of Leadership Wisdom

In the past a leader was a boss. Today's leaders must be partners with their people…They no longer can lead solely based upon positional power.

> Kenneth Blanchard

Smart people instinctively understand the dangers of entrusting our future to self-serving leaders who use our institutions…whether in the corporate or social sectors…to advance their own interests.

> Jim Collins

Sometimes, I think my most important job as CEO is to listen for bad news. If you don't act on it, your people will eventually stop bringing bad news to your attention and that is the beginning of the end.

> Bill Gates

Kindness is more powerful than compulsion.

> Charles Schwab

Leadership Wisdom from Business Leaders

Pay attention to those employees who respectfully ask why. They are demonstrating an interest in their jobs and exhibiting a curiosity that could eventually translate into leadership ability.

Harvey Mackay

Good leaders make people feel that they're at the very heart of things, not at the periphery. Everyone feels that he or she makes a difference to the success of the organization. When that happens people feel centered and that gives their work meaning.

Warren Bennis

The ability to deal with people is as purchasable a commodity as sugar or coffee and I will pay more for that ability than for any other thing under the sun.

John D. Rockefeller

If you see a snake, just kill it. Don't appoint a committee on snakes.

Ross Perot

Chapter 6

Leadership Wisdom from Sports Figures

The Little Book of Leadership Wisdom

It's what you learn after you know everything that counts.

> John Wooden

Leadership is unlocking people's potential to become better.

> Bill Bradley

Leadership is a matter of having people look at you and gain confidence, seeing how you react. If you're in control, they're in control.

> Tom Landry

To have long-term success as a coach or in any position of leadership, you have to be obsessed in some way.

> Pat Riley

Leadership Wisdom from Sports Figures

In a crisis, don't hide behind anything or anybody. They're going to find you anyway.

> Paul Bear Bryant

If you're not making mistakes, you're not trying hard enough.

> Vince Lombardi

Success comes from knowing that you did your best to become the best that you are capable of coming.

> John Wooden

Leadership is getting someone to do what they don't want to do, to achieve what they want to achieve.

> Tom Landry

Earn your leadership every day.

           Michael Jordan

Things turn out best for the people who make the best of the way things turn out.

            John Wooden

I don't know any other way to lead, but by example.

             Don Shula

My responsibility is getting all my players playing for the name on the front of the jersey and not on the back.

             Anonymous

Leadership Wisdom from Sports Figures

Be more concerned with your character than your reputation, because your character is what you really are, while your reputation is merely what others think you are.

John Wooden

You can observe a lot just by watching.

Yogi Berra

Build for your team a feeling of oneness, of dependence on one another, and of strength to be derived by unity.

Vince Lombardi

Leadership is an ever-evolving position.

Mike Krzyzewski

The Little Book of Leadership Wisdom

Leadership rests not only upon ability, not only upon capacity; having the capacity to lead is not enough. The leader must be willing to use it. His leadership is then based on truth and character. There must be truth in the purpose and will power in the character.

Vince Lombardi

Don't measure yourself by what you have accomplished, but by what you should have accomplished with your ability.

John Wooden

Paralyze resistance with persistence.

Woody Hayes

Leadership is diving for a loose ball, getting the crowd involved, getting other players involved. It's being able to take it as well as dish it out. That's the only way you're going to get respect from the players.

Larry Bird

Leadership Wisdom from Sports Figures

Leaders aren't born, they are made. And they are made just like anything else, through hard work. And that's the price we'll pay to achieve that goal, or any goal.

Vince Lombardi

If I have affected someone in a positive way, that means a lot to me.

Bill Parcells

The secret to success is good leadership, and good leadership is all about making the lives of your team members or workers better.

Tony Dungy

Setting a goal is not the main thing. It is deciding how you will go about achieving it and staying with that plan.

Tom Landry

Chapter 7

Leadership Wisdom from Literature and the Arts

The Little Book of Leadership Wisdom

The leader has to be practical and a realist, yet must talk the language of the visionary and the idealist.
>Eric Hoffer

Leaders make things possible. Exceptional leaders make them inevitable.
>Lance Morrow

One of the tests of leadership is the ability to recognize a problem before it becomes an emergency.
>Arnold H. Glasgow

Leaders conceive and articulate goals that lift people out of their petty preoccupations and unite them in pursuit of objectives worthy of their best efforts.
>John Gardner

Leadership Wisdom from Literature and the Arts

Leadership appears to be the art of getting others to want to do something you are convinced should be done.

                                      Vance Packard

The ability to summon positive emotions during periods of intense stress lies at the heart of effective leadership.

                                      Dr. Jim Loehr

Leadership is the ability to get extraordinary achievement from ordinary people.

                                      Brian Tracy

The world is starving for original and decisive leadership.

                                      Bryant H. McGill

The Little Book of Leadership Wisdom

The final test of a leader is that he leaves behind him in other men, the conviction and the will to carry on.

                                                Walter Lippman

---

A leader is one who knows the way, goes the way, and shows the way.

                                                John Maxwell

I start with the premise that the function of leadership is to produce more leaders, not more followers.

                                                Ralph Nader

A real leader faces the music even when he doesn't like the tune.

                                                Arnold H. Glasgow

Leadership Wisdom from Literature and the Arts

The leader is one who mobilizes others toward a goal shared by leaders and followers…Leaders, followers and goals make up the three equally necessary supports for leadership.

Gary Wills

A good general not only sees the way to victory; he also knows when victory is impossible.

Polybius

For every complex and difficult problem, there is an answer that is simple, easy, and wrong.

H. L. Mencken

A ruler should be slow to punish and swift to reward.

Ovid

The Little Book of Leadership Wisdom

The only real training for leadership is leadership.
>Antony Jay

Anyone can hold the helm when the sea is calm.
>Publilius Syrus

A great person attracts great people and knows how to hold them together.
>Johann Wolfgang Von Goethe

People buy into the leader before they buy into the vision.
>John Maxwell

Leadership Wisdom from Literature and the Arts

There is nothing more difficult to take in hand, more perilous to conduct, or more uncertain in its success than to take the lead in the introduction of a new order to things.

Niccolo Machiavelli

All leadership is influence.

John Maxwell

Leaders think and talk about the solutions. Followers think and talk about the problems.

Brian Tracy

A man who wants to lead the orchestra must turn his back on the crowd.

Max Lucado

A great leader's courage to fulfill his vision comes from passion, not position.

> John Maxwell

Leadership is particularly necessary to ensure ready acceptance of the unfamiliar and that which is contrary to tradition.

> Cyril Falls

Expect the best, plan for the worst, and prepare to be surprised.

> Dennis Waitley

Effective leadership is putting first things first. Effective management is discipline, carrying it out.

> Stephen Covey

Leadership Wisdom from Literature and the Arts

Management is efficiency in climbing the ladder of success; leadership determines whether the ladder is leaning against the right wall.

Steven Covey

If you're ridin ahead of the herd, take a look back every now and then to make sure it's still there.

Will Rogers

If at first you don't succeed, try, try again.

William Hickson

No one knows what they can do till they try.

Publilius Syrus

The Little Book of Leadership Wisdom

What you do has far greater impact than what you say.
>> Steven Covey

A good leader is a person who takes a little more than his share of the blame and little less than his share of the credit.
>> John Maxwell

Leadership consists not in degrees of technique, but in traits of character.
>> Lewis H. Lapham

Leadership is, among other things, the ability to inflict pain and get away with it short-term pain for long-term gain.
>> George Will

Leadership Wisdom from Literature and the Arts

Do not follow where the path may lead. Go instead where there is no path and leave a trail.

                                     Ralph Waldo Emerson

The pessimist complains about the wind. The optimist expects it to change. The leader adjusts the sails.

                                                 John Maxwell

---

I cannot give you the formula for success, but I can give you the formula for failure: which is: Try to please everybody.

                                                 Herbert Swope

---

The greater a man is in power above others, the more he ought to excel them in virtue. None ought to govern who is not better than the governed.

                                                 Publilius Syrus

High sentiments always win in the end; the leaders who offer blood, toil, tears and sweat always get more out of their followers than those who offer safety and a good time. When it comes to the pinch, human beings are heroic.

George Orwell

To command is to serve, nothing more and nothing less.

Andre Malraux

There is always room for a man of force, and he makes room for many. Society is a troop of thinkers, and the best heads among them take the best places.

Ralph Waldo Emerson

A chief is a man who assumes responsibility. He says, "I was beaten", he does not say "My men were beaten."

Antoine de Saint-Exupery

Leadership Wisdom from Literature and the Arts

Leadership involves finding a parade and getting in front of it.

John Naisbitt

The main thing is to keep the main thing the main thing.

Steven Covey

The majority of men meet with failure because of their lack of persistence in creating new plans to take the place of those which fail.

Napoleon Hill

It takes character and control to be understanding and forgiving.

Dale Carnegie

Our chief want is someone who will inspire us to be what we know we could be.
> Ralph Waldo Emerson

The people who get on in this world are the people who get up and look for the circumstances they want, and if they can't find them, make them.
> George Bernard Shaw

The key is not to prioritize what's on your schedule, but to schedule your priorities.
> Stephen Covey

Character matters; leadership descends from character.
> Rush Limbaugh

Leadership Wisdom from Literature and the Arts

If what you are doing is not moving you toward your goals, it is moving you away from your goals.
                                                      Brian Tracy

---

All of the great leaders have had one characteristic in common: it was the willingness to confront unequivocally the major anxiety of their people in their time. This, and not much else, is the essence of leadership.
                                   John Kenneth Galbraith

If you keeping doing what you've always done, you'll always get what you've always gotten.
                                           John Maxwell

Character is much easier kept than recovered.
                                           Thomas Paine

The Little Book of Leadership Wisdom

Don't judge each day by the harvest you reap, but by the seeds you plant.
>Robert Louis Stevenson

Nothing will ever be attempted if all possible objections must first be overcome.
>Samuel Johnson

A good leader is not the person who does things right, but the person who finds the right things to do
>Anthony T. Dadovano

Try not. Do or do not. There is no try.
>Yoda

Chapter 8

Leadership Wisdom from Scientists and Inventors

Sometimes we stare so long at a door that is closing that we see too late the one that is open.
> Alexander Graham Bell

The led must not be compelled; they must be able to choose their own leader.
> Albert Einstein

Example is not the main thing in influencing others; it is the only thing.
> Albert Schweitzer

Two things control men's nature, instinct and experience.
> Blaise Pascal

Leadership Wisdom from Scientists and Inventors

Insanity: doing the same thing over and over again and expecting different results.

Albert Einstein

Where there is shouting there is not true knowledge.

Leonardo da Vinci

Sometimes our light goes out, but it is blown into a flame by another human being. Each of us owes our deepest thanks to those who rekindle the flame.

Albert Schweitzer

Since we cannot know all that there is to be known about everything, we ought to know a little about everything.

Blaise Pascal

Genius is one percent inspiration and ninety-nine percent perspiration.
>
> Thomas Edison

Learn from yesterday; live for today; hope for tomorrow. The important thing is to not stop questioning.
>
> Albert Einstein

Success is not the key to happiness. Happiness is the key to success. If you love what you are doing, you will be successful.
>
> Albert Schweitzer

Give me a lever long enough and a fulcrum on which to place it, and I shall move the world.
>
> Archimedes

Leadership Wisdom from Scientists and Inventors

If we did all the things we are capable of doing, we would literally astound ourselves.

Thomas Edison

Try not to become a man of success, but rather try to become a man of value.

Albert Einstein

To every action there is always opposed an equal reaction.

Isaac Newton

Do something wonderful, people may imitate it.

Albert Schweitzer

A man, as a general rule, owes very little to what he is born with – A man is what he makes of himself.
>
> Alexander Graham Bell

No sensible decision can be made any longer without taking into account not only the world as it is, but the world as it will be.
>
> Isaac Asimov

We cannot solve our problems with the same thinking we used when we created them.
>
> Albert Einstein

It is surmounting difficulties that makes heroes.
>
> Louis Pasteur

Leadership Wisdom from Scientists and Inventors

You have to learn the rules of the game. And then you have to play better than anyone else.

Albert Einstein

Kind words do not cost much. Yet they accomplish much.

Blaise Pascal

Measure what is measurable, and make measurable what is not so.

Galileo Galilei

The first principle is that you must not fool yourself and you are the easiest person to fool.

Richard P. Feynman

A man should look for what is, and not for what he thinks should be.

> Albert Einstein

We cannot teach people anything; we can only help them to discover it within themselves.

> Galilei Galileo

There are three classes of people: those who see. Those who see when they are shown. Those who do not see.

> Leonardo da Vinci

The most valuable education of all is the ability to make yourself do the thing you have to do, when it has to be done, whether you like it or not.

> Aldous Huxley

Leadership Wisdom from Scientists and Inventors

A problem well stated is a problem half-solved.
>Charles Kettering

Our greatest weakness lies in giving up. The most certain way to succeed is always to try one more time.
>Thomas Edison

Make everything as simple as possible, but not simpler.
>Albert Einstein

The rung of a ladder was never meant to rest upon, but only to hold a man's foot long enough to enable him to put the other somewhat higher.
>Thomas Huxley

The Little Book of Leadership Wisdom

Experience is not what happens to you; it's what you do with what happens to you.
>Thomas Huxley

High achievement always takes place in the framework of high expectation.
>Charles F. Kettering

Fortune favors the prepared mind.
>Louis Pasteur

Tact is the art of making a point without making an enemy.
>Isaac Newton

Chapter 9

Leadership Wisdom from Proverbs

It is absurd that a man should rule others, who cannot rule himself.

> Latin Proverb

Not the cry, but the flight of a wild duck, leads the flock to fly and follow.

> Chinese Proverb

The same hammer that shatters the glass forges the steel.

> Russian Proverb

Tell me, and I'll forget. Show me, and I may not remember. Involve me, and I'll understand.

> Native American Proverb

Leadership Wisdom from Proverbs

The people follow the example of those above him.
> Chinese Proverb

Ask the experienced rather than the learned.
> Arabic Proverb

He who does nothing makes no mistakes.
> Italian Proverb

A man who thinks he is leading, but has no one following him is taking a walk.
> Chinese Proverb

The Little Book of Leadership Wisdom

Learning is a treasure that will follow its owner everywhere.

                                    Chinese Proverb

Lead, follow, or get out of the way.

                                    American Proverb

The obstacle is the path.

                                    Zen Aphorism

One step at a time is good walking.

                                    Chinese Proverb

Leadership Wisdom from Proverbs

He who is not satisfied with himself will grow; he who is not sure of his own correctness will learn many things.

Chinese Proverb

Practice what you preach.

Old English Proverb

The best leaders of all are the ones people do not know exist. They turn to each other and say, "We did it ourselves".

Zen Aphorism

The gem cannot be polished without friction nor man perfected without trials.

Chinese Proverb

Actions speak louder than words.
>Old English Proverb

If you are patient in one moment of anger, you will escape a hundred days of sorrow.
>Chinese Proverb

Fix the problem, not the blame.
>Japanese Proverb

Where there's a will, there's a way.
>Old English Proverb

Chapter 10

Other Leadership Wisdom

The Little Book of Leadership Wisdom

The very essence of leadership is that you have to have vision. You can't blow an uncertain trumpet.
> Theodore M. Hesburgh

You don't need a title to be a leader.
> Anonymous

Leadership is the key to ninety-nine percent of all successful efforts.
> Erskine Bowles

I don't know what leadership is. You can't touch it. You can't feel it. It's not tangible. But I do know this: you can recognize it when you see it.
> Bob Ehrilich

Other Leadership Wisdom

True leadership lies in guiding others to success. In ensuring that everyone is performing at their best, doing the work they are pledged to do and doing it well.

Bill Owens

I am endlessly fascinated that playing football is considered a training ground for leadership, but raising children isn't.

Dee Dee Meyers

Uncertainty is a permanent part of the leadership landscape. It never goes away

Andy Stanley

Leadership has been defined as the ability to hide your panic from others.

Anonymous

The Little Book of Leadership Wisdom

Whether a man is burdened by power or enjoys power; whether he is trapped by responsibility or made free by it; whether he is moved by other people and outer forces or moves them—this is the essence of leadership.
Theodore White

God, give us the grace to accept with serenity the things that cannot be changed, courage to change the things which should be changed, and the wisdom to distinguish the one from the other.
Reinhold Niebuhr

Leadership offers an opportunity to make a difference in someone's life, no matter what the project.
Bill Owens

Great leaders are not defined by the absence of weakness, but rather by the presence of clear strengths.
John Zenger

Other Leadership Wisdom

Because management deals mostly with the status quo and leadership deals mostly with change, in the next century we are going to have to try to become much more skilled at creating leaders.

John P. Kotter

Love and respect do not automatically accompany a position of leadership. They must be earned.

Anonymous

Leadership is about doing what you know is right – even when a growing din of voices around you is trying to convince you to accept what you know to be wrong.

Robert Ehrlich

Actions, not words, are the ultimate results of leadership.

Bill Owens

The Little Book of Leadership Wisdom

Our democracy poses problems and these problems must and shall be solved by courageous leadership.
 Charles Edison

I don't think leadership demands "yes" or "no" answers; I think leadership is providing the forum for making the right decision, which doesn't demand unanimity.
 Arthur Ochs Sulzberger, Jr.

The church wasn't an organization in the first century. They weren't writing checks or buying property. The church has matured and developed over the years. But for some reason, the last thing to change is the structure of leadership.
 Andy Stanley

The new leaders face new tests such as how to lead in this idea-intensive, interdependent network environment.
 John Scully

Other Leadership Wisdom

Uncertainty is not an indication of poor leadership; it underscores the need for leadership.

Andy Stanley

That is what leadership is all about: staking your ground ahead of where opinion is and convincing people, not simply following popular opinion of the moment.

Dorris Kearns Goodwin

A leader is a person who makes decisions. Sometimes they turn out right and sometimes they turn out wrong; but either way, the leader makes them.

Anonymous

The art of communication is the language of leadership.

James Humes

My philosophy of leadership is to surround myself with good people who have ability, judgment, and knowledge, but above all, a passion for service.

Sonny Perdue

Leaders instill in their people a hope for success and a belief in themselves. Positive leaders empower people to accomplish their goals.

Anonymous

Reason and calm judgment, the qualities specially belonging to a leader.

Tacitus

There are many qualities that make a great leader. But having strong beliefs, being able to stick with them through popular and unpopular times, is the most important characteristic of a great leader.

Rudolph Giuliani

Other Leadership Wisdom

Leadership is all about taking people on a journey. The challenge is that most of the time, we are asking people to follow us to places we ourselves have never been.

Andy Stanley

Leadership is intentional influence.

Anonymous

One secret of leadership is that the mind of a leader never turns off. Leaders, even when they are sightseers or spectators, are active; not passive observers.

James Humes

There is nothing inevitable about military victory, even for forces of apparently overwhelming strength. In the absence of inspired military leadership…the more powerful side wears down the weaker.

Bevin Alexander

Index

Adams, John Quincy,
sixth president of the United States
Agather, Elaine, American businesswoman
Alexander the Great, Macedonian king
Alexander, Bevin, American military historian
Aquinas, Thomas, Italian philosopher
Archimedes, Greek scientist
Aristotle, classical Greek philosopher
Ash, Mary Kay, founder of Mary Kay Cosmetics
Asimov, Isaac, American science author
Bacon, Sir Francis, English philosopher
Ballmer, Steve, Microsoft CEO
Bara, Hannibal, Punic Carthaginian military commander
Bell, Alexander Graham, American inventor
Bennis, Warren, American professor and author
Berra, Yogi, American baseball player
Bezos, Jeff, founder of Amazon
Bird, Larry, American basketball player
Blair, Tony, Prime Minister United Kingdom
Blanchard, Kenneth, American author
Bonaparte, Napoleon, French military and political leader
Bowles, Erskine, American businessman and politician

The Little Book of Leadership Wisdom

Bradley, Bill, American basketball player
Bradley, Omar N., American general
Branson, Sir Richard, founder of Virgin Group
Bryant, Paul Bear, American football coach
Buchan, John, governor general of Canada
Buffett, Warren, founder of Berkshire-Hathaway
Burke, Arleigh, United States admiral
Bush, George W.,
forty-third president of the United States
Carnegie, Andrew, American businessman
Carnegie, Dale, American author and speaker
Case, Steve, founder of AOL
Churchill, Winston, former British prime minister
Cicero, Marius Tullius, Roman philosopher
Clarke, Bruce C., American general
Confucius, Chinese philosopher
Conley, Chip, American hotelier and author
Covey, Steven, American author
Dadovano, Anthony T., American professor and author
Da Vinci, Leonardo, Italian painter
De Gaulle, Charles, French President
De Montaigne, Michel, French Renaissance writer
De Pree, Max, founder Herman Miller
Demosthenes, Greek statesman
Disney, Roy E., American businessman
Disraeli, Benjamin, former British prime minister
Drucker, Peter, author and management consultant
Dungy, Tony, American football player and coach

Index

Edison, Thomas, American inventor
Edison, Charles, American secretary of the navy
Ehrilich, Bob, governor of Maryland
Eisenhower, Dwight,
thirty-fourth president of the United States
Einstein, Albert, German physicist
Emerson, Ralph Waldo,
American essayist, poet and lecturer
Epicurus, ancient Greek philosopher
Euripides, classical Greek author and philosopher
Evenius, classic Greek author
Exupery, Antoine de Saint, Poet and aviation pioneer
Falls, Cyril, Irish historian
Feynman, Richard P., American physicist
Fields, Debbi, founder of Mrs. Field's
Firestone, Harvey S., founder of Firestone
Ford, Henry, founder of Ford
Franklin, Benjamin, American author and inventor
Galbraith, John Kenneth,
Canadian-American economist
Galilei, Galileo, Italian scientist
Gardner, John, American author
Gates, Bill, cofounder of Microsoft
Geneen, Harold, American businessman
Gertsner, Louis, CEO of IBM
Ghosn, Carlos, CEO of Nissan
Giuliani, Rudolph, New York mayor
Glasgow, Arnold H., American humorist

Goodwin, Doris Kearns, American author
Half, Robert, founder Robert Half
Hawken, Paul, founder of Smith Hawken
Hayes, Woody, college football coach
Heffernan, Margaret,
American businesswoman and writer
Heraclitus, Greek philosopher
Hesburgh, Theodore M., America priest
Hesiod, classical Greek poet
Hickson, William, British educational author
Hill, Napoleon, American author
Hock, Dee, founder and CEO Emeritus Visa
Hoffer, Eric, American philosopher
Hopper, Grace Murray, American rear admiral
Humes, James, American speechwriter
Huxley, Thomas, English biologist
Iacocca, Lee, American businessman
Illich, Ivan, Austrian philosopher
Iger, Bob, American businessman
Jackson, Andrew,
seventh president of the United States
Jobs, Steve, cofounder of Apple
Johnson, Samuel, English author
Jordan, Michael, American basketball player
Kamprad, Ingvar, founder IKEA
Kant, Immanuel, German philosopher
Keating, Paul, Australian prime minister
Kelleher, Herb, Southwest Airlines CEO

Index

Kennedy, John Fitzgerald,
thirty-fifth president of the United States
Kettering, Charles F., American inventor and engineer
Kissinger, Henry, American diplomat
Knight, Philip, founder Nike
Korn, Lester, American businessman
Kotter, John, American professor
Kroc, Ray, founder McDonalds
Krzyzewski, Mike, American basketball coach
Landry, Tom, American football coach
Lapham. Lewis H., American writer
Lee, Robert, E., Confederate general
Limbaugh, Rush, American talk radio show host
Lincoln, Abraham,
sixteenth president of the United States
Loehr, Dr. Jim, American psychologist
Lombardi, Vince, American football coach
Machiavelli, Niccolo, Italian historian and writer
Mackey, Harvey, American author and businessman
Malraux, Andre, French novelist
Marshall, George C., American general
Maxwell, John, American Christian author
MacArthur, Douglas, American general
McGannon, Donald H.,
American broadcasting executive
McGill, Bryant H., American author
McNealy, Scott, founder Sun Microsystems
Mencken, H. L., American journalist

The Little Book of Leadership Wisdom

Montgomery, Bernard, British field marshal
Morgan, J. P., American businessman
Mulcahy, Anne M., Xerox CEO
Naisbitt, John, American author
Newton, Isaac, English physicist
Niebuhr, Reinhold, American theologian
Nimitz, Chester W., American admiral
Nooyi, Indra, Indian-American business executive
Ogilvy, David, American businessman
Nunn, Sam, American senator
Orwell, George, English novelist
Owens, Bill, American congressman
Packard, Vance, American author
Paine, Thomas, English-American author
Parcells, Bill, American football coach
Pascal, Blaise, French mathematician
Pasteur, Louis, French chemist and microbiologist
Patton, George S., US general
Penney, J.C., founder J.C. Penney
Perdue, Sonny, governor of Georgia
Peters, Tom, American consultant and author
Perot, Ross, American businessman
Pershing, John J., American general
Pickens, T. Boone, American businessman
Plato, Greek philosopher
Polybius, Greek historian
Porter, Michael, Harvard professor and author
Powell, Colin, American secretary of state

Index

Queen Elizabeth II, queen of England
Reagan, Ronald, fortieth president of the United States
Ridgway, Matthew B., American general
Riley, Pat, American basketball player and executive
Rockefeller, J.D., American industrialist and philanthropist
Rohn, Jim, American author and entrepreneur
Romney, Mitt, governor of Massachusetts
Roosevelt, Franklin D.,
thirty-second president of the United States
Roosevelt, Theodore,
twenty-sixth president of the United States
Rubio, Marco, United States senator
Rumsfeld, Donald,
American politician and businessman
Santayana, George, Spanish philosopher
Schwab, Charles, American businessman
Schwarzkopf, Norman, American army general
Schultz, Howard, founder of Starbucks
Seneca, Lucius Annaeus, Roman philosopher
Sculley, John, Pepsi and Apple CEO
Senge, Peter, American scientist
Shula, Don, American football coach
Smith, Fredrick, founder FedEx
Socrates, classical Greek philosopher
Stanley, Andy, American pastor
Stockdale, James B., American admiral
Sulzberger, Arthur Ochs, Jr,
American newspaper publisher

Swope, Herbert, journalist
Syrus, Publilius, Latin writer
Tacitus, Roman senator
Theophrastus, Greek teacher and philosopher
Thompson, Daley, British Olympic athlete
Thoreau, Henry David, American author
Tracy, Brian, American author
Truman, Harry,
thirty-third president of the United States
Trump, Donald, American businessman
Tzu, Sun, ancient Chinese military strategist
Voltaire, French author
Waitley, Dennis, motivational speaker and writer
Walton, Sam, founder of Wal-Mart
Washington, George, first American president
Watson, Thomas J., founder IBM
Welch, Jack, GE CEO
White, Theodore, political journalist
Whitman, Meg, Ebay and HP CEO
Will, George, American journalist
Wills, Gary, American author
Wilson, Woodrow,
twenty-eighth president of the United States
Wooden, John, American basketball player and coach
Yoda, Grand Master of the Jedi Council, from *Star Wars*
Zenger, John, German American journalist

About the Author

Charles D. (Dan) Harpool began his business career when he started his first business when he was ten years old. He has worked in numerous marketing and management positions in the corporate world. Dan also has extensive experience in small and medium-size organizations including entrepreneurial endeavors over his long career in the business world.

Dan earned a Bachelor's degree in Marketing and Management and a Master's degree in Business Administration from Missouri State University in Springfield, Missouri. Dan is the President and CEO of Complete Computing, a networking solutions and IT services provider. Dan serves on numerous boards, conducts seminars on strategic planning and provides strategic planning consulting services for profit and non-profit organizations. Dan is the author of *The Little Book of Planning Wisdom* available at www.amazon.com in print and Kindle versions.

Contact Dan at cdharpool@gmail.com. On Twitter @danharpool. Dan Harpool on both Facebook and LinkedIn. Or www.danharpoolconsulting.com.

Made in the USA
Columbia, SC
24 July 2023